THE FESTIVALS OF INDIA

A CULTURAL AND SPIRITUAL GUIDE TO INDIA'S CELEBRATIONS

DR. JAGADEESH PILLAI

Made with ♥ on the Notion Press Platform
www.notionpress.com

|| "Dedicated to all who seek to understand and appreciate Indian culture and tradition." ||

Contents

Contents

PRAYER

"Om Bhadram Karnebhih Shrunuyaama DevaahBhadram Pashyemaakshabhiryajatraah SthiraiangaistushtuvaamsastanoobhihVyashema Devahitam YadaayuhSwasti Na Indro VridhashravaahSwasti Nah Pooshaa VishwavedaahSwasti Nastaarkshyo ArishtanemihSwasti No Brihaspatir DadhaatuOm Shantih, Shantih, Shantih"

The literal meaning of this mantra is: OM. O Gods! Let us hear auspicious words from our ears. O reverent Gods! Let us behold propitious visions from our eyes, let our organs and body be stable, healthy, and strong. Let us do that which is pleasing to the gods in the life span allotted to us. May Indra, inscribed in the scriptures, bring us fortune! May Pushan, the knower of the world, grant us prosperity! May Trakshya, who vanquishes enemies, bestow us with blessings! May Brihaspati bring us success!
OM Peace, Peace, Peace.

About The Author

Dr. Jagadeesh Pillai is a renowned Guinness World Record holder, writer, and researcher hailing from Varanasi, also known as the abode of Lord Shiva. With a Ph.D. in Vedic Science and a range of creative ideas and achievements, he is a true polymath. He is the author of more than 100 books including Research Publications. Although his roots can be traced back to Kerala, the people of Varanasi hold him in high regard and affectionately consider him one of their own.

Dr. Pillai has achieved four Guinness World Records in the following subjects:

"Script to Screen" - In this record, Dr. Pillai produced and directed an animation film within the shortest time possible, breaking the previous record set by Canadians. He has also received numerous national and international awards and recognitions for this achievement.

Longest Line of Postcards - For this record, Dr. Pillai created a line of 16,300 postcards on the occasion of the 163rd anniversary of Indian Postal Day. The event also included a questionnaire about the Indian flag.

Largest Poster Awareness Campaign - Dr. Pillai designed an awareness campaign on the subject of "Beti Bachao - Beti Padhao" (Save the Girl Child - Educate the Girl Child) to achieve this record.

Largest Envelope - In tribute to the Indian Prime Minister's

"Make in India" initiative, Dr. Pillai created a 4000 square meter envelope using waste paper to achieve this record.

Attempted - **70000 Candles on a 210 kg Cake** - To celebrate the 70th Indian Independence Day, Dr. Pillai attempted to light 70,000 candles on a 210 kg cake, which was recorded in World Records India.

Attempted - **Documentary on Dhamek Stupa of Sarnath in 17 Languages** - Dr. Pillai attempted to create a documentary on the Dhamek Stupa of Sarnath, dubbing it in 17 different languages. The result of this attempt is currently awaiting confirmation from the Guinness World Records.

Dr. Pillai is skilled in teaching the Bhagavad Gita, a Hindu scripture, and is popular among young people. He has helped many young people improve their lives through his motivational teachings.

In addition to teaching, he has composed and sung numerous Sanskrit Bhajans and patriotic songs.

He has also written and directed several short films and documentaries for awareness campaigns, and has volunteered with the police in both UP and Kerala to spread awareness about various issues through videos and photography.

Incredibly, he has produced and directed over 100 documentaries about the city of Varanasi, all on his own.

He has also helped and guided more than 25 boys and girls to achieve world records through creative and innovative methods. He is a multifaceted person who uses his intellect and the blessings given to him by God to excel in various areas. He is both a teacher and a student, always learning and teaching, and is able to master any subject he comes across.

He is a selfless social activist and motivational speaker who has overcome struggles and failures to become a successful and enthusiastic individual with a rich life experience.

In addition to his work with the Bhagavad Gita, he is also an efficient Tarot card reader, Astro-Vastu consultant, and a talented singer and composer. He has sung the entire Ram Charita Manas and Bhagavad Gita in his own compositions, and has sung the phrase "Lokah Samastha Sukhino Bhavantu" in 50 different languages. He is currently working on a detailed and scientific study of Vedas, Upanishads, Puranas, and the Bhagavad Gita. He has also composed and sung the Hanuman Chalisa and Gayatri Mantra in 108 and 1008 different compositions, respectively.

Awards - Four Times Guinness World Records, Winner of Mahatma Gandhi Vishwa Shanti Puraskar, Mahatma Gandhi Global Peace Ambassador, Kashi Ratna Award, Dr. APJ Abdul Kalam Motivational Person of the Year 2017, Mother Teresa Award, Indira Gandhi Priyadarshini Award, Bharat Vikas Ratna Award, Udyog Ratna Award, Vigyan Prasar Award, Poorvanchal Ratn Samman.

PREFACE

The Festivals of India: A Cultural and Spiritual Guide to India's Celebrations is a comprehensive look at the rich tapestry of festivals that are celebrated in India. From the bright colors and music of Holi to the solemnity of Gurpurab, this book delves deep into the history, significance and celebrations of some of the most popular and important festivals in India.

India is a land of diverse cultures, religions, and traditions, and this diversity is reflected in the numerous festivals that are celebrated throughout the year. This book aims to provide an understanding of the various festivals and their significance in Indian culture and society, and how these festivals are an essential part of Indian life.

Through this book, we will explore the history and philosophy behind each festival, its rituals and customs, and its significance to the people of India. We will also take a look at the regional variations of each festival, and how it is celebrated differently across the country.

This book is not only for those who are looking to understand the cultural and spiritual significance of Indian festivals, but also for anyone interested in learning about the diversity and richness of Indian culture. It will be an invaluable resource for scholars, students, and travelers alike.

So, join us as we embark on a journey through the Festivals of India: A Cultural and Spiritual Guide to India's

Celebrations, and discover the vibrant and colorful world of Indian festivals.

I

Significance of Festivals in Indian Culture

India is a land of festivals, where every month, every season, and every reason is celebrated with great fervor and enthusiasm. These festivals are not just about celebrations and gaiety, but also about preserving and promoting the cultural and spiritual heritage of India.

The festivals of India are rooted in ancient traditions, and many of them have religious or spiritual significance. For example, Diwali, the festival of lights, is a Hindu festival that marks the victory of good over evil, and is celebrated by lighting diyas and candles, and exchanging sweets and gifts. Similarly, Eid al-Fitr, the festival that marks the end of the holy month of Ramadan, is celebrated by Muslims with great fervor and enthusiasm.

In addition to religious festivals, India also celebrates many secular festivals, such as Independence Day and Republic Day, which commemorate important national events. These festivals are an opportunity for people to come together, regardless of their religious or cultural backgrounds, to celebrate the unity and diversity of India.

Festivals in India also provide an opportunity for people to come together and celebrate their cultural heritage. Many festivals involve traditional music, dance, and art, and are an opportunity for people to experience and appreciate the rich cultural heritage of India.

Yes, festivals in India play a significant role in preserving and promoting the cultural and spiritual heritage of India. They are an opportunity for people to come together, regardless of their religious or cultural backgrounds, to celebrate and appreciate the unity and diversity of India. From religious festivals to secular celebrations, the festivals of India are an integral part of the country's cultural heritage, and offer a unique and exciting experience for anyone who wants to discover the traditions and customs of India.

"Indian festivals are a celebration of life and its many colors."

II

Diwali: The Festival of Lights

Diwali, also known as the "festival of lights," is one of the most important and widely celebrated festivals in India. It is a Hindu festival that marks the victory of good over evil, and is celebrated by lighting diyas and candles, and exchanging sweets and gifts.

The festival of Diwali is celebrated in the Hindu month of Ashwin, which usually falls in October or November. The celebration lasts for five days, and each day has its own significance. On the first day, known as Dhanteras, people worship the goddess of wealth, Laxmi, and purchase new items for their homes. The second day is Narak Chaturdashi, where people worship Lord Vishnu and Lord Shiva to get rid of their sins. The third day is the main day of Diwali, where people light diyas and candles, and exchange sweets and gifts with loved ones. The fourth day is Govardhan Puja, where people worship Lord Krishna and the fifth day is Bhai Dooj, where brothers and sisters exchange gifts.

Diwali is celebrated across India and around the world, and has become an important festival for the Indian diaspora. In India, people decorate their homes with lights, rangolis, and flowers, and prepare traditional sweets and savories to share with family and friends. Fireworks displays are also a common feature of Diwali celebrations.

Diwali has a spiritual significance, as it marks the victory of light over darkness, and symbolizes the triumph of good over evil. It is an opportunity for people to let go of their past mistakes and to start anew, with a clean slate.

Diwali is one of the most important and widely celebrated festivals in India. It is a Hindu festival that marks the victory of good over evil, and is celebrated by lighting diyas and candles, and exchanging sweets and gifts. The festival is celebrated across India and around the world, and has spiritual significance as it symbolizes the triumph of good over evil. The festival of Diwali is celebrated in the Hindu month of Ashwin and is a five-day celebration each day having its own significance.

"The diversity of Indian festivals reflects the diversity of its people and culture."

III

Holi: The Festival of Colors

Holi, also known as the "festival of colors," is one of the most popular and widely celebrated festivals in India. It is a Hindu festival that marks the arrival of spring and the end of winter. The festival is celebrated on the full moon day in the Hindu month of Phalguna, which usually falls in February or March.

The highlight of Holi is the throwing of colored powders and water, also known as "gulal," on friends and family. People also light bonfires and sing and dance around them to celebrate the arrival of spring and the victory of good over evil.

Holi also has a religious significance, as it marks the story of the demon king Hiranyakashyap and his son Prahlada, who was a devout follower of Lord Vishnu. Hiranyakashyap wanted his son to worship him instead of Lord Vishnu, but

Prahlada refused. In anger, Hiranyakashyap tried to kill his son, but Lord Vishnu protected him, ultimately killing the demon king. Holi is celebrated to mark the victory of Prahlada and the triumph of good over evil.

Traditionally, people also prepare special sweets and delicacies for Holi such as gujiya, mathri, dahi bhalla, and thandai. The festival is celebrated with great enthusiasm and joy all over India, and has become an important festival for the Indian diaspora.

Holi is a Hindu festival that marks the arrival of spring and the end of winter, celebrated by throwing of colored powders and water, also known as "gulal," on friends and family, lighting bonfires and sing and dance around them. It has a religious significance, as it marks the victory of good over evil, and the story of Prahlada and Lord Vishnu. The festival is celebrated with great enthusiasm and joy all over India and it's also an important festival for the Indian diaspora. The festival is usually celebrated in the Hindu month of Phalguna and is a two day festival.

"Indian festivals bring people together, breaking down barriers and fostering unity."

IV

Navratri: The Festival of Nine Nights

Navratri, also known as "the festival of nine nights," is one of the most important and widely celebrated festivals in India. It is a Hindu festival that honors the goddess Durga, who is believed to have defeated the demon king Mahishasura. The festival is celebrated for nine consecutive nights and ten days, usually in September or October.

Each night of Navratri is dedicated to a different form of the goddess Durga, and people perform puja (worship) and offer prayers to her. The ninth night, known as "Mahanavami" or "Navami," is considered the most important and is celebrated with great fervor and devotion.

Navratri is also a time of fasting, where people abstain from eating meat, and some also abstain from consuming any type of food. Many people also perform the Garba and Dandiya dance, which is a traditional dance form that originated in Gujarat.

The festival is also associated with fasting and abstinence, and many people fast for the entire duration of Navratri. Some also perform the Garba and Dandiya dance, which is a traditional dance form that originated in Gujarat, during the festival.

Navratri is a Hindu festival that honors the goddess Durga, celebrated for nine consecutive nights and ten days. Each night is dedicated to a different form of the goddess Durga, and people perform puja and offer prayers to her. The festival is associated with fasting and abstinence, many people fast for the entire duration of Navratri.

It's also a time when people perform the Garba and Dandiya dance, which is a traditional dance form that originated in Gujarat. Navratri is celebrated in September or October every year, and is an important festival in many parts of India.

"In India, festivals are not just a time for celebration, but also a time for reflection and renewal."

V

Durga Puja: The Celebration of the Divine Feminine

Durga Puja, also known as "Durgotsav," is one of the most important and widely celebrated festivals in India, particularly in the states of West Bengal, Odisha, Assam and Tripura. It is a Hindu festival that honors the goddess Durga, who is considered the embodiment of the divine feminine and the destroyer of evil. The festival typically takes place in September or October, and lasts for five to ten days.

During Durga Puja, large and elaborately decorated statues of the goddess Durga are installed in pandals (temporary structures) and are worshiped with offerings of flowers, fruits, and sweets. The festival is also marked by traditional music and dance performances, as well as community meals.

Durga Puja is considered one of the most significant festivals in Bengali culture, and is an opportunity for people to come together and celebrate the divine feminine. It is also believed to bring good luck and prosperity, and people seek blessings from the goddess for a successful and happy life.

In addition to the religious significance, Durga Puja is also celebrated as a cultural festival, where people come together to celebrate the vibrant culture and traditions of Bengal. The festival is also known for its elaborate and colorful pandals, which are decorated with intricate themes, and for the "Sarbojanin" (community) puja where the community, regardless of caste, class or religion, come together to celebrate the festival.

Durga Puja is a Hindu festival that honors the goddess Durga, celebrated particularly in the states of West Bengal, Odisha, Assam and Tripura. It typically takes place in September or October, and lasts for five to ten days. During the festival, large and elaborately decorated statues of the goddess Durga are installed in pandals and are worshiped with offerings of flowers, fruits, and sweets.

The festival is also marked by traditional music and dance performances, as well as community meals. It's considered one of the most significant festivals in Bengali culture and is an opportunity for people to come together and celebrate the divine feminine, culture and traditions of Bengal.

"Indian festivals are a reminder of the rich history and traditions of the country."

VI

Ramnavami: The Birth of Lord Rama

Ramnavami is a Hindu festival that celebrates the birth of Lord Rama, the seventh avatar of Lord Vishnu. It is typically celebrated in the Hindu month of Chaitra (March or April) on the ninth day of the Shukla Paksha (the bright lunar fortnight).

The festival is celebrated with great devotion and reverence, with people fasting and performing puja (worship) to Lord Rama. Many temples dedicated to Lord Rama hold special puja and katha (narrative) recitations, and people also read the Ramayana, the epic poem that tells the story of Lord Rama's life.

Ramnavami is also marked by processions and chariot (Rath Yatra) celebrations, where devotees pull chariots bearing Lord Rama's statue through the streets, accompanied by music and chants of "Jai Sri Ram" (Victory to Lord Rama).

The festival is especially significant in the northern and western states of India, and in Nepal, where Lord Rama is considered a symbol of righteousness and virtue. It is also celebrated by the Jain community, who believe that Lord Rama was the last Tirthankara of the present age.

In addition to its religious significance, Ramnavami is also celebrated as a cultural festival, with people dressing in traditional clothes, preparing special foods, and participating in cultural programs and competitions.

Ramnavami is a Hindu festival that celebrates the birth of Lord Rama, typically celebrated in the Hindu month of Chaitra on the ninth day of the Shukla Paksha. It is celebrated with great devotion and reverence, with people fasting and performing puja to Lord Rama. Many temples hold special puja and katha recitations, and people also read the Ramayana.

The festival is marked by processions and chariot celebrations, and is especially significant in the northern and western states of India, and in Nepal. It is also celebrated by the Jain community as the last Tirthankara of the present age. The festival also has cultural significance with people dressing in traditional clothes, preparing special foods and participating in cultural programs and competitions.

"The vibrant colors and joyous celebrations of Indian festivals are a feast for the senses."

VII

Ganesh Chaturthi: The Festival of Lord Ganesha

Ganesh Chaturthi, also known as "Vinayaka Chaturthi," is a Hindu festival that celebrates the birth of Lord Ganesha, the elephant-headed god of wisdom and remover of obstacles. The festival typically takes place in the Hindu month of Bhadrapada, which falls in August or September, and lasts for ten days.

During the festival, large and elaborately decorated statues of Lord Ganesha are installed in homes and public pandals (temporary structures) and are worshiped with offerings of flowers, fruits, and sweets. The festival is also marked by traditional music and dance performances, as well as community meals.

On the last day of the festival, the statues are taken out in a grand procession and immersed in a nearby water body, symbolizing the lord's return to the divine.

Ganesh Chaturthi is especially significant in the state of Maharashtra, where it originated, and is widely celebrated across India and around the world, particularly by the Indian diaspora. It is considered an auspicious occasion and is believed to bring good luck and prosperity.

In addition to its religious significance, Ganesh Chaturthi is also celebrated as a cultural festival, with people participating in cultural programs and competitions, such as Rangoli and Modak making.

Ganesh Chaturthi is a Hindu festival that celebrates the birth of Lord Ganesha, typically taking place in the Hindu month of Bhadrapada and lasting for ten days. During the festival, large and elaborately decorated statues of Lord Ganesha are installed in homes and public pandals and are worshiped with offerings of flowers, fruits, and sweets. The festival is marked by traditional music and dance performances, as well as community meals.

On the last day, the statues are taken out in a grand procession and immersed in a nearby water body. The festival is especially significant in the state of Maharashtra and is widely celebrated across India and around the world, particularly by the Indian diaspora. It is considered an auspicious occasion and is celebrated not just for religious significance but also as a cultural festival.

"Indian festivals are a celebration of the cycle of life and death, and the connection between the two."

VIII

Onam: The Festival of Harvest in Kerala

Onam is a major festival celebrated in the southern Indian state of Kerala, which marks the beginning of the harvest season. It is typically celebrated in August or September, and lasts for ten days.

The festival is celebrated to honor the legendary King Mahabali, who is said to have ruled Kerala during a golden age of prosperity and equality. Onam is celebrated in his honor, with the belief that he returns to his kingdom during the festival to see the well-being of his people.

During Onam, people decorate their homes and streets with colorful floral arrangements called "pookalam," and prepare traditional foods and sweets, such as payasam and sadya, to share with family and friends. The festival is also marked by traditional music and dance performances, as well as boat races and sports competitions.

Onam is considered the state festival of Kerala, and is widely celebrated by people of all religions and communities. It is a time of great joy and celebration, and is an opportunity for people to come together to give thanks for the bountiful harvest and to pray for continued prosperity.

In addition to its religious significance, Onam is also celebrated as a cultural festival, with people participating in traditional games and competitions, such as Onathallu (wrestling), Onapottan (masked dance), and Onam Kali (stick fight).

Onam is a major festival celebrated in the southern Indian state of Kerala, which marks the beginning of the harvest season, typically celebrated in August or September and lasting for ten days. The festival is celebrated to honor the legendary King Mahabali, with the belief that he returns to his kingdom during the festival to see the well-being of his people.

During Onam, people decorate their homes and streets with colorful floral arrangements, prepare traditional foods and sweets, and participate in traditional music and dance performances, as well as boat races and sports competitions. It is considered the state festival of Kerala and widely celebrated by people of all religions and communities. It is a time of great joy and celebration and is also celebrated as a cultural festival, with people participating in traditional games and competitions.

"The diversity of Indian festivals is a reflection of the country's diverse religions and communities."

IX

Pongal: The Festival of Harvest in Tamil Nadu

Pongal is a major festival celebrated in the southern Indian state of Tamil Nadu, which marks the beginning of the harvest season. It is typically celebrated in January, and lasts for four days.

The festival is celebrated to give thanks for the bountiful harvest, and to pray for continued prosperity. It is also a time to honor the Sun God, who is considered the giver of all life and energy, and the cows, which are considered sacred animals in Hinduism.

During Pongal, people decorate their homes and streets with colorful decorations, and prepare traditional foods and sweets such as Pongal, a sweet dish made from rice, milk and jaggery. The festival is also marked by traditional music and dance performances, as well as sports competitions, such as Jallikattu, a traditional bull-taming event.

Pongal is considered the most important festival in Tamil Nadu, and is widely celebrated by people of all religions and communities. It is a time of great joy and celebration, and is an opportunity for people to come together to give thanks for the bountiful harvest and to pray for continued prosperity.

In addition to its religious significance, Pongal is also celebrated as a cultural festival, with people participating in traditional games and competitions, such as Kambam, traditional sports like Kambattam, and Kolam, a traditional form of drawing patterns with rice flour.

Pongal is a major festival celebrated in the southern Indian state of Tamil Nadu, which marks the beginning of the harvest season, typically celebrated in January and lasting for four days. The festival is celebrated to give thanks for the bountiful harvest and to pray for continued prosperity. It is also a time to honor the Sun God, and cows which are considered sacred animals. During Pongal, people decorate their homes and streets with colorful decorations, and prepare traditional foods and sweets.

The festival is marked by traditional music and dance performances, as well as sports competitions such as Jallikattu. Pongal is considered the most important festival in Tamil Nadu and is widely celebrated by people of all religions and communities. It is also celebrated as a cultural festival, with people participating in traditional games and competitions.

"Indian festivals are a way for people to come together and celebrate their shared culture and heritage."

X

Dussehra: The Victory of Good over Evil

Dussehra, also known as "Vijayadashami," is a major Hindu festival that celebrates the victory of good over evil. It is typically celebrated in September or October, and lasts for ten days.

The festival commemorates the victory of Lord Rama, an incarnation of Lord Vishnu, over the demon king Ravana, as told in the Hindu epic Ramayana. It marks the triumph of good over evil and is seen as a victory of righteousness over injustice.

During Dussehra, large and elaborately decorated effigies of Ravana, his brother Kumbhakarna and son Meghanath are burnt in a symbolic representation of the defeat of evil. The festival is also marked by traditional music and dance performances, as well as community meals and shared feasts.

Dussehra is celebrated across India, but is particularly significant in northern and western India, where Lord Rama is considered a symbol of righteousness and virtue. It is also an important festival in Nepal, where it is celebrated as "Dashain."

In addition to its religious significance, Dussehra is also celebrated as a cultural festival, with people participating in traditional games and competitions, such as Ramlila, a dramatic reenactment of the Ramayana, and Dussehra Mela, a fair.

Dussehra, also known as "Vijayadashami," is a major Hindu festival that celebrates the victory of good over evil, typically celebrated in September or October and lasting for ten days. The festival commemorates the victory of Lord Rama over the demon king Ravana, as told in the Hindu epic Ramayana, and marks the triumph of good over evil. During Dussehra, large and elaborately decorated effigies of Ravana, his brother Kumbhakarna and son Meghanath are burnt in a symbolic representation of the defeat of evil, and the festival is also marked by traditional music and dance performances, as well as community meals and shared feasts.

It is celebrated across India, but is particularly significant in northern and western India, where Lord Rama is considered a symbol of righteousness and virtue, and is also an important festival in Nepal, where it is celebrated as "Dashain." The festival is also celebrated as a cultural festival, with people participating in traditional games and competitions, such as Ramlila and Dussehra Mela.

"The bright lights and lively music of Indian festivals create a joyous and festive atmosphere."

XI

Buddha Purnima: The Celebration of Buddha's Birth

Buddha Purnima, also known as Vesak, is a major Buddhist festival that celebrates the birth, enlightenment, and passing away of Gautama Buddha. It is typically celebrated in April or May, and is one of the most important festivals in Buddhism.

Buddha Purnima marks the anniversary of the birth of Gautama Buddha, who is considered the founder of Buddhism. It is a time to reflect on the teachings of Buddha, and to celebrate his life and legacy.

During Buddha Purnima, Buddhists engage in a variety of rituals and practices, such as visiting temples and monasteries, making offerings to statues of the Buddha, and participating in prayer and meditation. Many people also engage in acts of charity and service, such as feeding the poor or helping the community.

The festival is widely celebrated across Asia, with large-scale celebrations in countries such as India, Nepal, Sri Lanka, China, and Japan. It is also celebrated by Buddhist communities around the world.

In addition to its religious significance, Buddha Purnima is also celebrated as a cultural festival, with people participating in traditional music and dance performances, and other cultural activities.

Buddha Purnima, also known as Vesak, is a major Buddhist festival that celebrates the birth, enlightenment, and passing away of Gautama Buddha. It is typically celebrated in April or May and is one of the most important festivals in Buddhism. It marks the anniversary of the birth of Gautama Buddha, who is considered the founder of Buddhism. During Buddha Purnima, Buddhists engage in a variety of rituals and practices, such as visiting temples and monasteries, making offerings to statues of the Buddha, and participating in prayer and meditation.

The festival is widely celebrated across Asia, with large-scale celebrations in countries such as India, Nepal, Sri Lanka, China, and Japan, it is also celebrated by Buddhist communities around the world. It is also celebrated as a cultural festival, with people participating in traditional music and dance performances, and other cultural activities.

"Indian festivals are a symbol of the country's resilience and ability to overcome challenges."

XII

Sikh Festivals: Vaisakhi and Gurpurab

Vaisakhi and Gurpurab are two of the most important festivals in Sikhism.

Vaisakhi, also known as Baisakhi, is a festival that marks the Sikh New Year, and the beginning of the solar calendar. It is celebrated on April 13th or 14th, and is a time of great joy and celebration for Sikhs. During Vaisakhi, people attend special prayers at gurdwaras (Sikh temples), and participate in processions and parades, known as Nagar Kirtan. It is also a time to reflect on the teachings of the Sikh Gurus, and to celebrate the formation of the Khalsa, the community of initiated Sikhs.

Gurpurab, also known as "the festival of the Guru," is a series of festivals that commemorate the birth and martyrdom of the Sikh Gurus. The most important gurpurab is the one celebrating the birthday of Guru Nanak, the founder of Sikhism, which is celebrated on the full moon day in the month of Kartik (October/November). During Gurpurab, people attend special prayers at gurdwaras, listen to hymns and kirtans, and participate in langar, a communal meal.

Both Vaisakhi and Gurpurab are important religious and cultural celebrations for Sikhs, and are a time for people to come together to remember the teachings of the Sikh Gurus and to celebrate the Sikh community.

Vaisakhi and Gurpurab are two of the most important festivals in Sikhism. Vaisakhi, also known as Baisakhi, marks the Sikh New Year, and the beginning of the solar calendar and is celebrated on April 13th or 14th. During Vaisakhi, people attend special prayers at gurdwaras (Sikh temples) and participate in processions and parades known as Nagar Kirtan. Gurpurab, also known as "the festival of the Guru," is a series of festivals that commemorate the birth and martyrdom of the Sikh Gurus, the most important gurpurab is the one celebrating the birthday of Guru Nanak, the founder of Sikhism, which is celebrated on the full moon day in the month of Kartik (October/November). During Gurpurab, people attend special prayers at gurdwaras, listen to hymns and kirtans, and participate in langar, a communal meal. Both Vaisakhi and Gurpurab are important religious and cultural celebrations for Sikhs and are a time for people to come together to remember the teachings of the Sikh Gurus and to celebrate the Sikh community.

"The many different festivals celebrated in India show the rich tapestry of its culture and society."

XIII

Makar Sankranti - Kite Festival

Makar Sankranti, also known as the Kite Festival, is a major festival celebrated in North India, marking the beginning of the sun's journey into the northern hemisphere. It is observed on January 14th every year and is celebrated in various ways across different states in North India, with kite flying being a common thread that connects the celebrations.

The festival is celebrated to mark the end of the winter solstice and the start of the sun's journey towards the northern hemisphere. It is considered an auspicious day, and is associated with the harvest season, making it a festival of great significance for farmers. People thank the Sun God for a good harvest and pray for a bountiful one in the coming year.

One of the most popular ways of celebrating Makar

Sankranti in North India is by flying kites. People of all ages participate in kite flying, with the skies filled with brightly colored kites of all shapes and sizes. Kite flying competitions are also organized, with prizes for the best kites and the most skilled kite flyers.

Another important aspect of Makar Sankranti is the consumption of khichdi, a dish made of rice and lentils. It is considered a sacred food, and is said to have been consumed by the sages during ancient times. It is also believed to have medicinal properties and is a comforting food during the cold winter months. People consume it on the day of Makar Sankranti, and it is also distributed among friends and family as a symbol of love and togetherness.

In Gujarat, Makar Sankranti is celebrated as Uttarayan and is one of the biggest festivals of the state. It is celebrated over two days, with the first day being dedicated to kite flying, and the second day is dedicated to prayer and religious rituals. People participate in kite flying competitions and a huge fair is organized in Ahmedabad, the state capital, where people gather to buy kites and other items.

In Maharashtra, Makar Sankranti is celebrated as Sankrant, and is celebrated as a harvest festival. People thank the Sun God for a good harvest and pray for a bountiful one in the coming year. People also consume sweets made from jaggery and sesame seeds, and visit the local temples to offer prayers.

In North India, Makar Sankranti is a festival that brings

people together, breaking down barriers of caste, class, and religion. It is a festival that celebrates the cycle of nature and the changing of seasons, and is a time for people to come together and celebrate the bounties of nature. It is a time to reflect on the past year and to look forward to the new one with hope and optimism.

Makar Sankranti is a major festival celebrated in North India, marking the beginning of the sun's journey into the northern hemisphere. It is observed on January 14th every year and is celebrated in various ways across different states in North India, with kite flying being a common thread that connects the celebrations. It is an auspicious day, and is associated with the harvest season, making it a festival of great significance for farmers. People thank the Sun God for a good harvest and pray for a bountiful one in the coming year. The festival is also known for its consumption of khichdi, a dish made of rice and lentils, which is considered sacred and is said to have medicinal properties.

The festival is celebrated differently across North India, with Gujarat and Maharashtra having their own unique way of celebrating the festival. But what connects all the celebration is the kite flying, people of all ages participate in kite flying, with the skies filled with brightly colored kites of all shapes and sizes. In Gujarat, the festival is celebrated over two days, with the first day being dedicated to kite flying, and the second day is dedicated to prayer and religious rituals. In Maharashtra, people consume sweets made from jaggery and sesame seeds, and visit the local temples to offer prayers. Makar Sankranti is a festival that brings people together, breaking down barriers of caste, class, and religion, it is a time to reflect on the past year and to look forward to the new one with hope and optimism.

"Indian festivals are a celebration of the cycle of the seasons, and the changing of the year."

XIV

Eid al-Fitr and Eid al-Adha: the Islamic Festivals

Eid al-Fitr and Eid al-Adha are two of the most important festivals in the Islamic calendar.

Eid al-Fitr, also known as "the Festival of Breaking the Fast," marks the end of the holy month of Ramadan, during which Muslims fast from sunrise to sunset. It is celebrated on the first day of the Islamic month of Shawwal, and is typically a three-day celebration. During Eid al-Fitr, Muslims attend special prayers, give zakat (charity) to the poor, and visit family and friends. It is also a time of great joy and celebration, marked by the exchange of gifts and festive meals.

Eid al-Adha, also known as "the Festival of Sacrifice," commemorates the willingness of the prophet Ibrahim

(Abraham) to sacrifice his son as an act of obedience to God. It is celebrated on the tenth day of the Islamic month of Dhu al-Hijjah, and is typically a four-day celebration. During Eid al-Adha, Muslims perform the Hajj pilgrimage to Mecca, if they are able, and also slaughter an animal, usually a sheep, and distribute the meat to the poor and needy. It is also a time of great joy and celebration, marked by the exchange of gifts and festive meals.

Both Eid al-Fitr and Eid al-Adha are important religious and cultural celebrations for Muslims worldwide, and are a time for people to come together to give thanks to God, to celebrate and reflect on their faith, and to strengthen community ties.

Eid al-Fitr and Eid al-Adha are two of the most important festivals in the Islamic calendar. Eid al-Fitr marks the end of the holy month of Ramadan, and is celebrated on the first day of the Islamic month of Shawwal, typically a three-day celebration. During Eid al-Fitr, Muslims attend special prayers, give zakat to the poor, and visit family and friends. Eid al-Adha commemorates the willingness of prophet Ibrahim to sacrifice his son, and is celebrated on the tenth day of the Islamic month of Dhu al-Hijjah, typically a four-day celebration. During Eid al-Adha, Muslims perform the Hajj pilgrimage to Mecca, if they are able, and also slaughter an animal and distribute the meat to the poor and needy. Both festivals are important religious and cultural celebrations for Muslims worldwide, and are a time for people to come together to give thanks to God, to celebrate and reflect on their faith, and to strengthen community ties.

"The delicious food and sweet treats of Indian festivals are a celebration of the country's rich culinary traditions."

XV

Christmas: India's Christian Festivals

Christmas, also known as "the Nativity of Jesus Christ," is a major Christian festival that celebrates the birth of Jesus Christ. It is celebrated on December 25th by Christians all over the world, including India.

In India, Christmas is celebrated by Christians of all denominations, including Roman Catholics, Protestants, and Anglicans. On Christmas Eve, churches hold special services, known as "Midnight Mass," to commemorate the birth of Jesus. On Christmas Day, people attend church services, exchange gifts, sing carols, and decorate their homes with Christmas trees, lights, and other decorations.

Christmas is a time of great joy and celebration for Christians in India, and is an opportunity for people to come together to remember the birth of Jesus and the message of hope, peace, and love that it represents. It is also a time to reflect on one's faith and to strengthen community ties.

In addition to its religious significance, Christmas is also celebrated as a cultural festival, with people participating in traditional games and competitions, such as carol singing, and Christmas fairs, as well as traditional foods like Christmas pudding, and Christmas cakes.

Christmas, also known as "the Nativity of Jesus Christ," is a major Christian festival that celebrates the birth of Jesus Christ, it is celebrated on December 25th by Christians all over the world, including India. In India, it is celebrated by Christians of all denominations and is a time of great joy and celebration. On Christmas Eve, churches hold special services known as "Midnight Mass" and on Christmas Day people attend church services, exchange gifts, sing carols, and decorate their homes.

It is a time to reflect on one's faith, to strengthen community ties and also celebrated as a cultural festival, with people participating in traditional games and competitions, such as carol singing, and Christmas fairs, as well as traditional foods like Christmas pudding, and Christmas cakes.

"The deep spiritual meaning behind Indian festivals is a reminder of the country's rich spiritual heritage."

XVI

Chhath Puja of North India

Chhath Puja is one of the most major festivals of India and Nepal, celebrated by the people of the state of Bihar, Uttar Pradesh, and some parts of Nepal. It is a festival that is dedicated to the worship of the Sun God, Surya, and his wife, Chhathi Maiya. This festival is celebrated twice a year, once during the month of Chaitra (April-May) and again during the month of Kartik (October-November).

The festival is celebrated over a period of four days, with the main rituals taking place on the fourth day. The rituals begin with the 'Nahai-Khai' ceremony, where devotees take a dip in the river or a pond, and offer prayers to the setting sun. The next day is known as 'Kharna', where devotees observe a fast and prepare offerings for the Sun God. On the third day, known as 'Sandhya Arghya', devotees offer prayers to the rising sun and make offerings of fruits, sweets, and coconuts. The fourth day is known as 'Usha

Arghya', and is the main day of the festival. On this day, devotees make offerings of prasad and arghya to the setting sun, and offer prayers for the well-being of their family and friends.

One of the most unique aspects of Chhath Puja is the 'Arghya' ceremony, where devotees make offerings of prasad and arghya to the setting sun. The arghya is made of fruits, sweets, and coconuts, and is placed in a bamboo basket, which is then floated in the river or a pond. The devotees then offer prayers and sing hymns, asking for the blessings of the Sun God.

Another important aspect of Chhath Puja is the 'Vratt', which is a vow that is taken by the devotees. The Vratt is a promise to observe a fast and to perform the rituals of the festival for the well-being of their family and friends. The Vratt is usually taken by women, and is considered a way to show devotion and gratitude to the Sun God.

Chhath Puja is one of the most major festivals of India and Nepal, celebrated by the people of the state of Bihar, Uttar Pradesh, and some parts of Nepal. It is a festival that is dedicated to the worship of the Sun God, Surya, and his wife, Chhathi Maiya. This festival is celebrated twice a year, over a period of four days, with the main rituals taking place on the fourth day. One of the unique aspects of the festival is the 'Arghya' ceremony, where devotees make offerings of prasad and arghya to the setting sun and the 'Vratt' which is a vow taken by the devotees for the well-being of their family and friends. The festival is a way to show devotion and gratitude to the Sun God.

OTHER BOOKS OF THE AUTHOR

1. The Moments When I Met God
2. Kashiyile Theertha Pathangal
3. GURU GYAN VANI
4. Abhiprerak Gita
5. ASSI SE JAIN GHAT TAK
6. Hopelessness of Arjuna
7. The Soul and It's True Nature
8. Sense of Action (Karma)
9. Action through Wisdom
10. Action through Wisdom
11. THEORY AND PRACTICAL OF EVERY ACTION
12. LOGICAL UNDERSTANDING OF THE SUPREME
13. THE IMPERISHABLE SUPREME
14. Yatra Nishadraj se Hanuman Ghat Tak
15. Yatra Karnatak Ghat se Raja Ghat Tak
16. Yatra Pandey Ghat se Prayagraj Ghat Tak
17. Yatra Ranjendra Prasad Ghat se Dattatreya Ghat Tak
18. YaatraSindhiya Ghat se Gwaliar Ghat Tak
19. Yatra Mangala Gauri Ghat se Hanuman Gadhi Ghat Tak
20. Yatra Gaay Ghat Se Nishad Ghat Tak
21. MAA GANGA, GHATEN EVM UTSAV
22. Ganga Arti Dev Deepavali evam Any Utsav
23. Potentials of Digitalized India
24. VEDIC CONSCIOUSNESS
25. A Brief Introduction to Vedic Science
26. Kashi ke Barah Jyotirling
27. IMPACT OF MOTIVATION
28. Let's have a Milky Way Journey
29. Color Therapy in a Nutshell

30. Rigveda in a Nutshell
31. Yajurveda in a Nutshell
32. Samveda in a Nutshell
33. Atharva Veda in a Nutshell
34. Ayushman Bhava - Ayurveda
35. Srimad Bhagavad Gita and Upanishad Connection
36. Srimad Bhagavad Gita - an attempt to summarize each chapter.
37. Facts and Impact of Nakshatra
38. Astro Gems - NAVARATNA
39. Ekadashi - A Concise Overview
40. A Concise View of Hanuman Chalisa
41. Inspirational Gita
42. Nakshatraranyam
43. Summary of 18 Mahapuranas
44. Synopsis of 18 Upa Puranas
45. Rigvediya Upanishads
46. Shukla Yajurvediya Upanishads
47. Krishna Yajurvediya Upanishads
48. Samavediya Upanishads
49. Atharvavediya Upanishads
50. The Seven Great Sages
51. From Rocket Scientist to President Dr. APJ Abdul Kalam
52. The Visionary's Voice - Quotes of Dr. APJ Abdul Kalam
53. The Wisdom of Swami Vivekananda: Insights and Inspiration from a Legendary Spiritual Teacher
54. Ayurvedic Remedies from the Garden
55. Sages and Seers
56. Rising Strong – Motivational Stories of Women
57. Beyond Flames -Mystery stories of Funeral Ghat Manikarnika
58. The Origins of Tulsi: A Look at the Mythological Roots of the Plant"

59. The Holistic Cow: A Look at the Physical, Spiritual, and Cultural Importance of Cows in India
60. Arts of Healing
61. Exploring the Divine
62. Understanding Five Elements
63. The Etymology of Ram
64. Symbols of India
65. Voice of Change (About Speeches of Great Men)
66. She Speaks (About Speeches of Great Women)
67. **Patriotism on Celluloid – Brief About Patriotic Films**
68. **The Music of Motivation: A Brief Guide to Inspirational Film Songs**
69. **Unlocking the Secrets of the Dashopanishads**
70. A Cultural Mosaic
71. Ancient Traditions, Modern Minds
72. Ecos of Ancient Wisdom
73. Beneath the Surface
74. From Temples to Ashrams
75. Sages of the Subcontinent
76. The Art of Healling (Ayurveda, Yoga & Naturopathy)
77. Indian Kitchen

CONTACT

DR. JAGADEESH PILLAI

PhD in Vedic Science

Four Times Guinness World Record Holder

Winner of Mahatma Gandhi Vishwa Shanti Puraskar and Global Peace Ambassador

Gemology, Astro & Vastu Consultant - Spiritual Counselor

Consultant for designing World Record Ideas

Efficient Tarot Card Reader

9839093003

myrichindia@gmail.com

drjagadeeshpillai@facebook

drjagadeeshpillai@instagram

jagadeeshpillai@youtube

www. JAGADEESHPILLAI.com

|| LOKAHA SAMSTHAHA SUKHINO BHAVANTU ||

9 798889 511335

Printed by Libri Plureos GmbH in Hamburg, Germany